human
body

Conceived and produced by Weldon Owen Pty Ltd
59–61 Victoria Street, McMahons Point
Sydney NSW 2060, Australia

Copyright © 2008 Weldon Owen Pty Ltd

WELDON OWEN GROUP
Chairman John Owen

WELDON OWEN PTY LTD
Chief Executive Officer Sheena Coupe
Creative Director Sue Burk
Publisher Margaret Whiskin
Senior Vice President, International Sales Stuart Laurence
Vice President, Sales and New Business Development Amy Kaneko
Vice President Sales: Asia and Latin America Dawn Low
Administration Manager, International Sales Kristine Ravn
Production Manager Todd Rechner
Publishing Coordinator Mike Crowton

Consultant Dr Robin Arnold
Designer Jacqueline Richards

ISBN: 978-1-921530-01-2

Color reproduction by (SC) San Choy International Pte Ltd
Printed by SNP Leefung Printers Ltd
Manufactured in China 5 4 3 2 1

A WELDON OWEN PRODUCTION

encyclopedia of the

human
body

Robert Coupe

WELDON OWEN

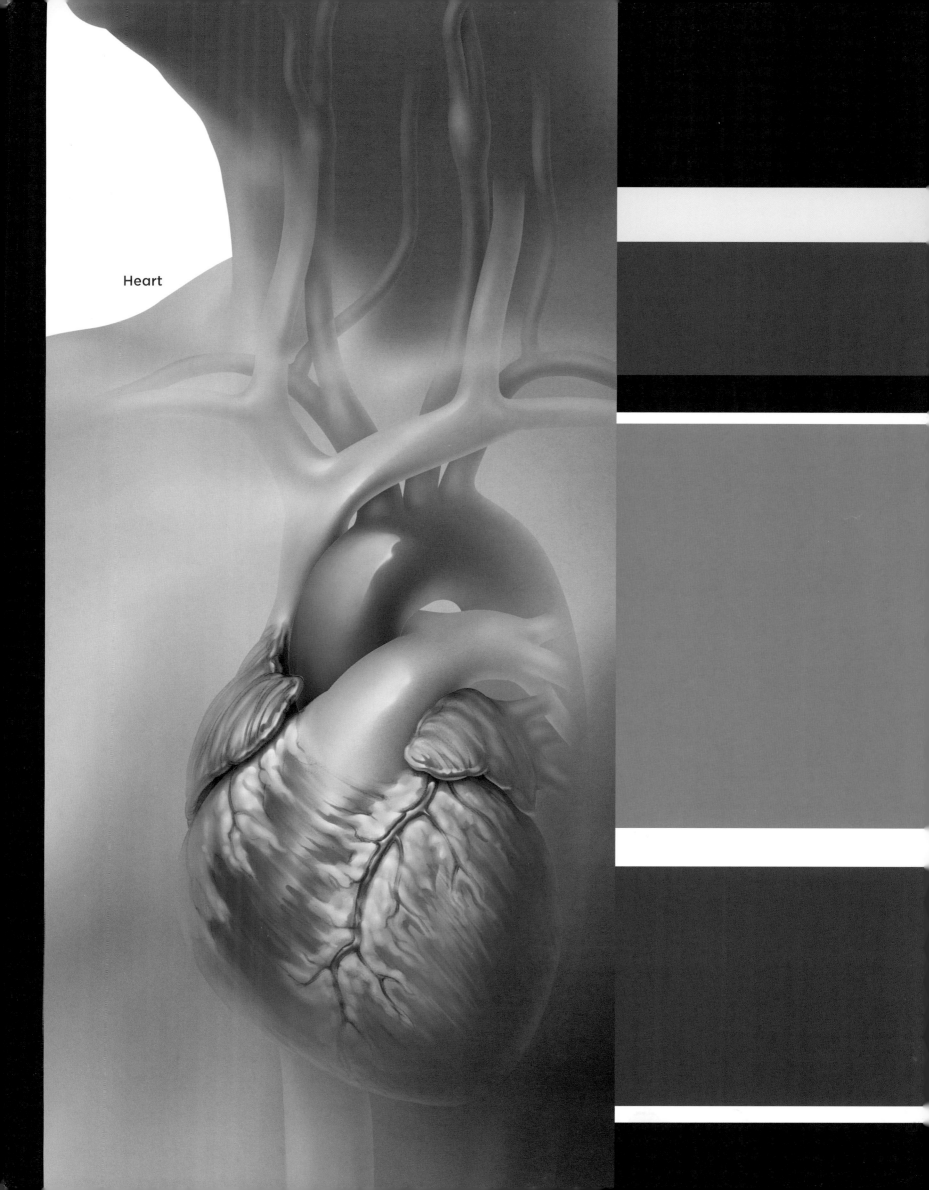

Heart

contents

Our amazing bodies

Our bodies are like complicated machines. Different parts have separate jobs to do. When all parts of your body are working well, your body is healthy. When something goes wrong with one or more parts, you can get sick. Doctors now have a good understanding of how our bodies work and know how to cure many kinds of sickness.

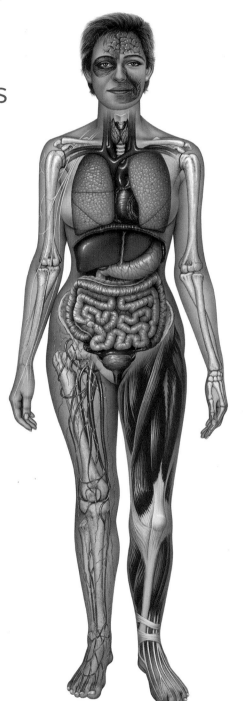

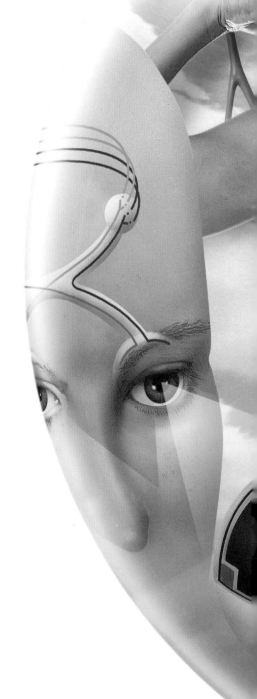

Seeing inside

If you could look inside a human body, this is what you would see. How many inside parts can you name?

Looking inside

About 500 years ago, doctors first began cutting up dead bodies to find out how the different parts worked.

Many parts

In this book, you will learn all about your body. You will understand what each part does and how to keep fit and well.

The smallest bits

Every living thing is made up of cells. Cells are the smallest parts of all plants, animals, and human beings. Your body contains about 100 million separate cells. They are like tiny factories that never stop working to keep your body healthy and energetic.

Different cells

There are about 200 different kinds of cells in your body. They control different parts of your body.

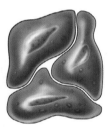

Skin cells

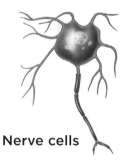

Nerve cells

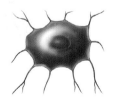

Bone cells

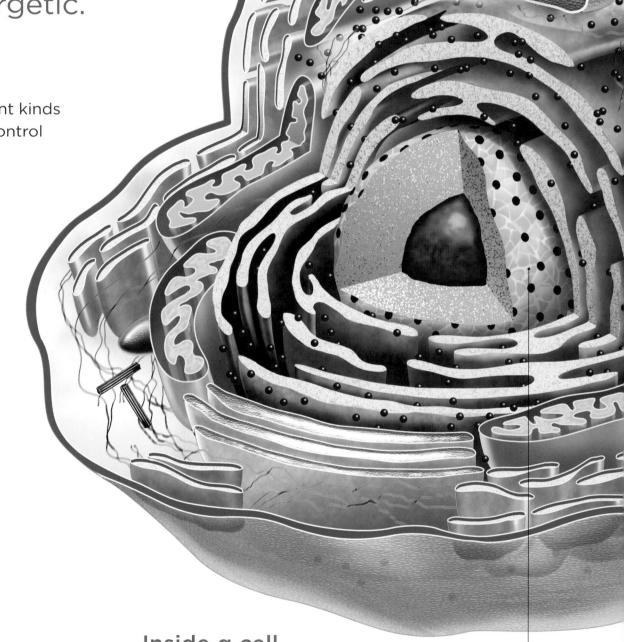

Inside a cell

A cell has many parts. The outside part is called a membrane. The center part is called a nucleus.

Nucleus

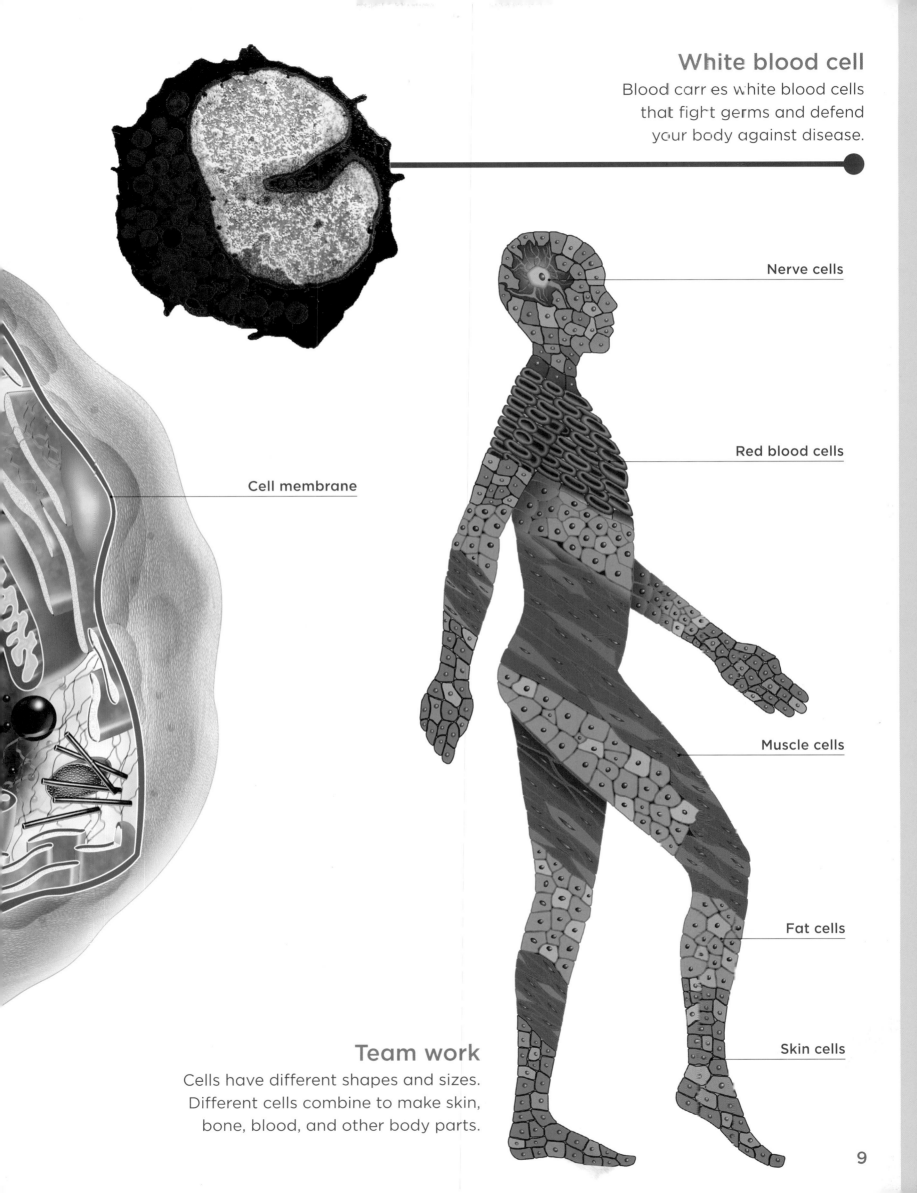

White blood cell
Blood carries white blood cells that fight germs and defend your body against disease.

Nerve cells

Red blood cells

Cell membrane

Muscle cells

Fat cells

Team work
Cells have different shapes and sizes. Different cells combine to make skin, bone, blood, and other body parts.

Skin cells

Our body covering

Your skin protects the inside parts of your body. Almost every time you move, some skin falls off. New skin grows to take its place. The outside part of your skin is the epidermis. Underneath is the thicker dermis. Hair grows through your skin. Sweat comes out through pores in your skin.

Fingerprints

Fingerprints are the patterns of skin on your fingertips. Every person's fingerprints are different.

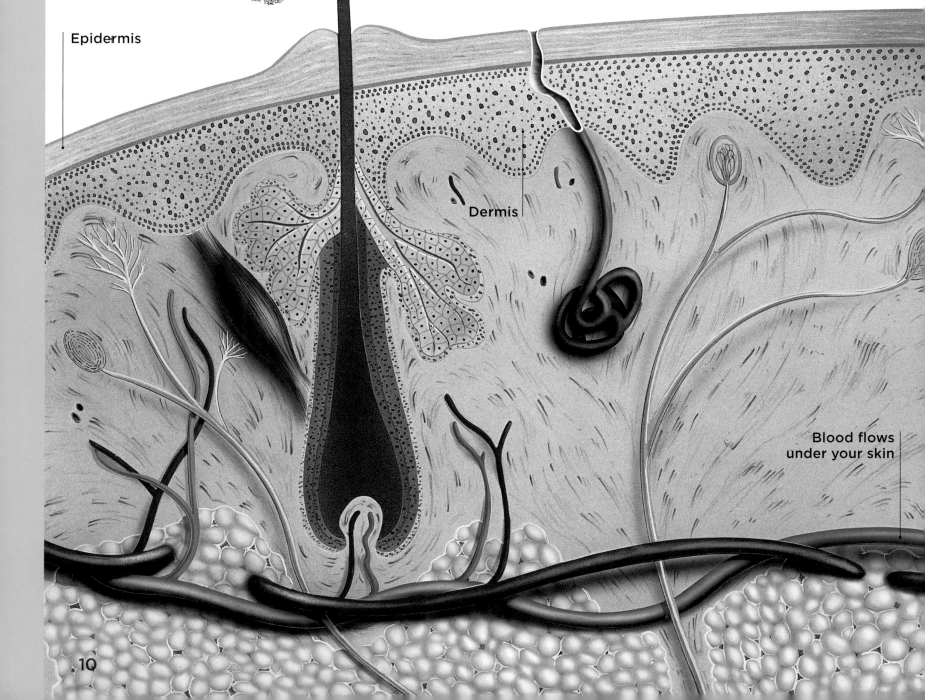

Epidermis

Dermis

Blood flows under your skin

Thinner and thicker

The skin on your fingertips is thin. Skin on your knuckles is thicker and has more wrinkles.

Knuckle

Fingertip

Cold skin
When you are cold your skin goes paler. Blood leaves the skin and goes to deeper organs.

Hot skin
When you are hot, your skin sweats. This helps to cool your body down.

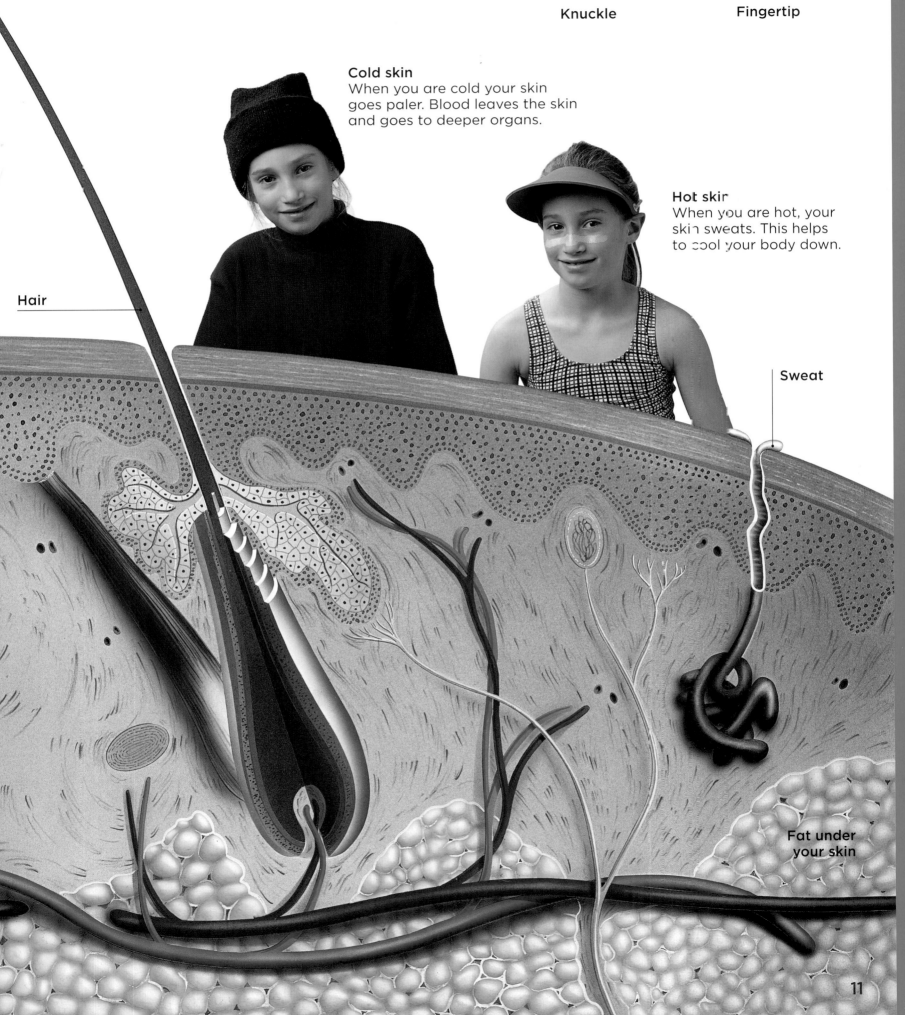

Hair

Sweat

Fat under your skin

Hair and nails

Hair grows over most parts of your body. It grows out through tiny holes in your skin. Most of this hair is soft and very short. The hairs in your ears and nose help stop germs getting in. Nails protect soft parts of your fingers and toes.

Changing color
Melanin colors your hair and your skin. As people get older, their hair stops making melanin, and it turns white or gray.

Head hair
Hair grows most thickly on your head. It protects your scalp from the rays of the hot sun and helps keep your head warm in winter.

Curly, wavy, or straight?

Hair can have different shapes. That is why some people have curly hair, some have straight hair, and others have hair that is wavy.

Curly hair

Wavy hair

Straight hair

Toes and fingers

Nails grow from roots in the skin of your fingers and toes. This picture shows the layers of skin, bone, and fat in a finger.

Nail

Skin

Fat

Root of nail

Bone

Teeth

Your teeth are covered with enamel. This is the hardest substance in your body. Your teeth need to be hard to do all the work of tearing, chomping, mashing, and grinding the food you eat. They also help protect the rest of your mouth against blows and knocks.

Different shapes, different jobs

The wide, sharp incisor teeth at the front of your mouth are for cutting and biting. Next to them, the pointed canines tear and rip food. Farther back, the flatter premolars and molars do the chewing and crushing work.

Incisor   Canine   Premolar   Molar

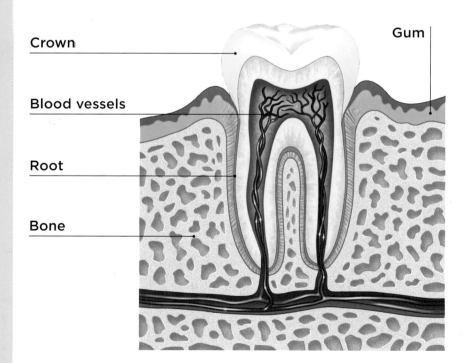

Crown

Blood vessels

Root

Bone

Gum

Parts of a tooth

Teeth grow out of your gums. A tooth's root is underneath the gum, surrounded by bone. The crown is the part above the gum.

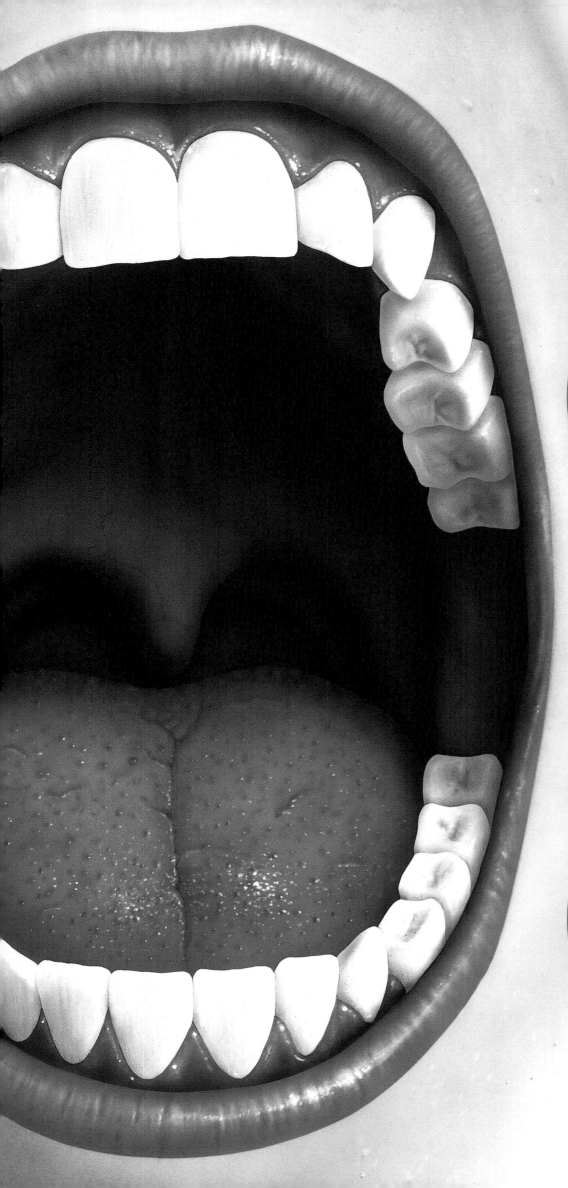

Working together

While your teeth bite and chew your food, your cheeks help to squeeze and squash it. Your tongue moves it around in your mouth, and then pushes it down into your throat.

Teeth problems

Sometimes teeth grow crooked or have big gaps between them. Braces on your teeth can fix problems like these.

Bones and skeletons

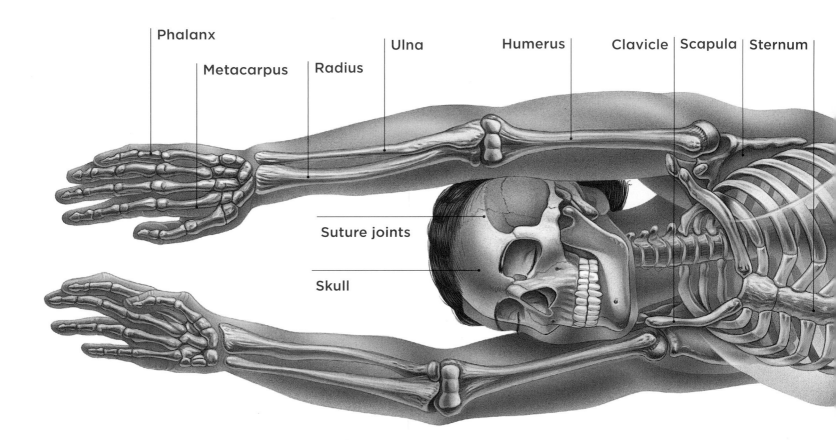

Phalanx
Metacarpus
Radius
Ulna
Humerus
Clavicle
Scapula
Sternum
Suture joints
Skull

Your bones are strong and hard. All the bones in your body make up your skeleton. Without them, you would be soft and floppy, and would not be able to stand and move around. Some bones also help protect and guard the inside parts of your body.

Different bones

Bones have special names. About half of all your bones are the small ones in your hands, wrists, ankles, and feet.

Inside a bone

A bone is like a tube. The outside part is hard. Inside is a soft and spongy substance called marrow.

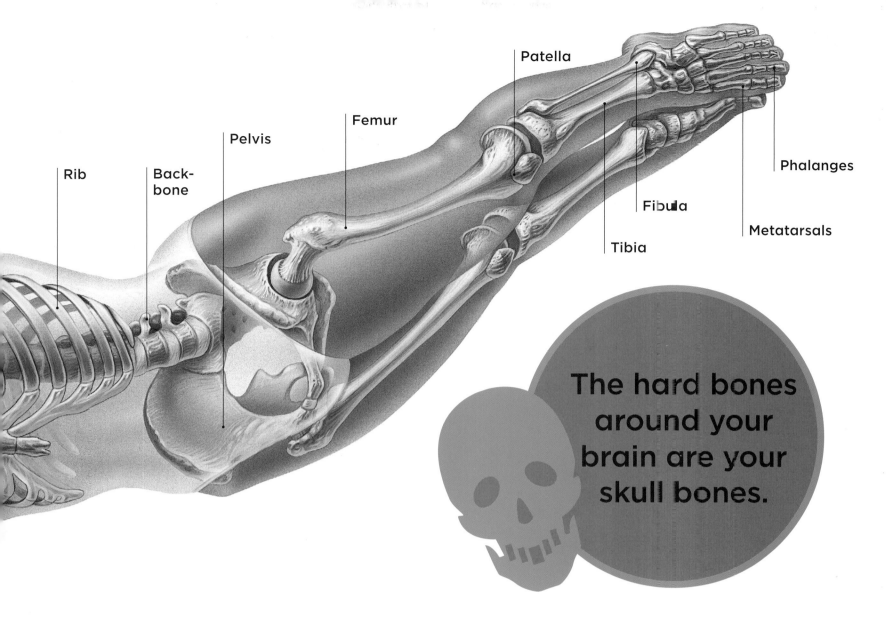

Rib

Back-bone

Pelvis

Femur

Patella

Phalanges

Fibula

Metatarsals

Tibia

The hard bones around your brain are your skull bones.

Broken bones

Broken bones grow back together. A plaster cast holds them in place so that they grow straight.

Muscles

Every time you move, you use muscles. Muscles allow you to blink, jump, run, talk, and sing. They also help you to eat and digest food. Many muscles inside your body work by themselves. You cannot control them. The muscles you can control are attached to your bones. We call these skeletal muscles.

Building muscles

If you don't use your muscles, they get weaker and smaller. Exercise helps to keep your muscles strong.

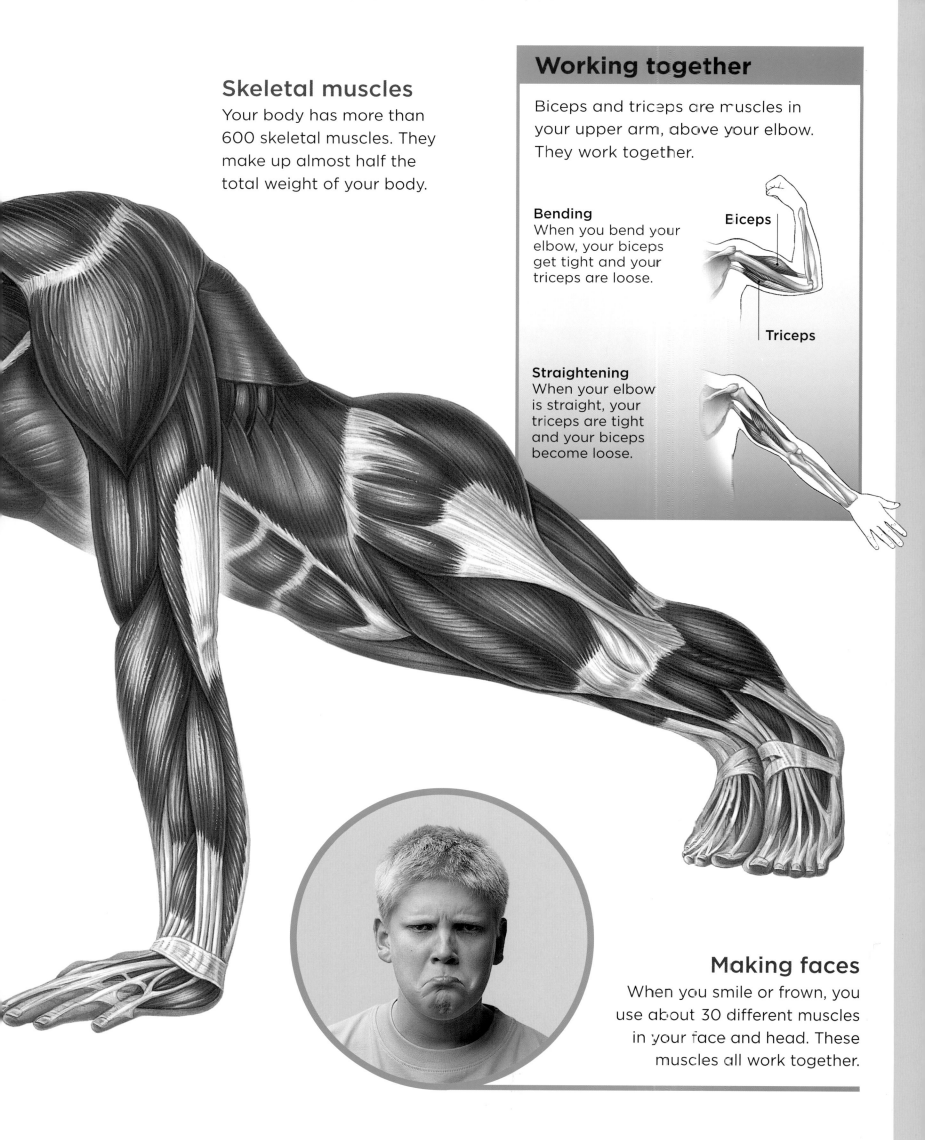

Skeletal muscles

Your body has more than 600 skeletal muscles. They make up almost half the total weight of your body.

Working together

Biceps and triceps are muscles in your upper arm, above your elbow. They work together.

Bending
When you bend your elbow, your biceps get tight and your triceps are loose.

Biceps

Triceps

Straightening
When your elbow is straight, your triceps are tight and your biceps become loose.

Making faces

When you smile or frown, you use about 30 different muscles in your face and head. These muscles all work together.

movement and exercise

Exercise is good for our bodies. Running, walking, swimming, and other kinds of movement help make us strong, fit, and healthy. When we move around, we bend our arms, legs, ankles, fingers, and toes. Our bones do not bend. There are joints between the bones. These allow bones to move up and down or from side to side.

People run fast, but cheetahs can run much faster.

Find the joints

When you ride a skateboard, your joints let you bend and move many bones in your body. How many joints can you see in this picture?

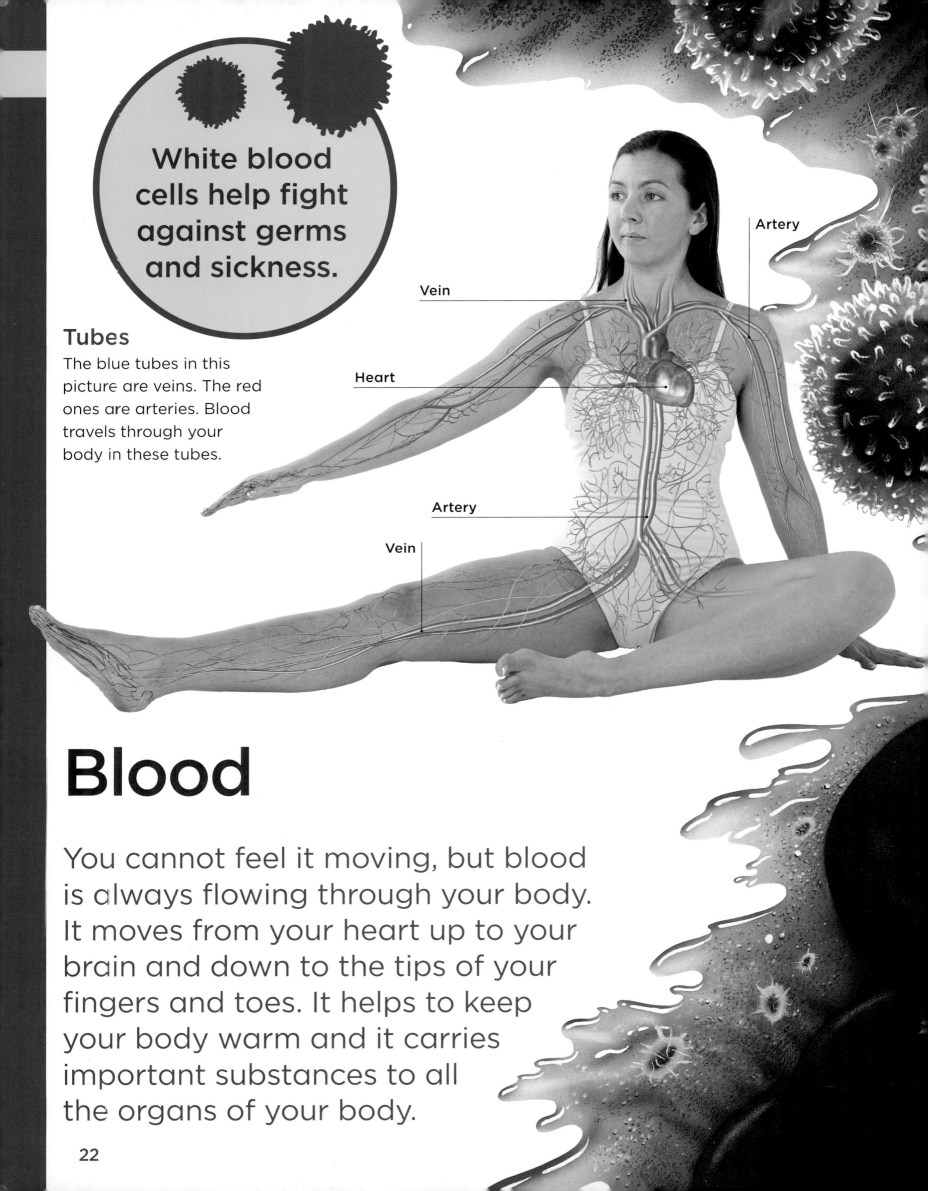

White blood cells help fight against germs and sickness.

Tubes

The blue tubes in this picture are veins. The red ones are arteries. Blood travels through your body in these tubes.

Vein

Artery

Heart

Artery

Vein

Blood

You cannot feel it moving, but blood is always flowing through your body. It moves from your heart up to your brain and down to the tips of your fingers and toes. It helps to keep your body warm and it carries important substances to all the organs of your body.

White cell

Cells

There are trillions of blood cells in your body. Most of them are red cells. A much smaller number are white cells.

Red cell

More about blood

You can see the veins in the inside of your wrist. Sometimes, these veins look blue. Veins and arteries are blood vessels. Other blood vessels are much tinier tubes, called capillaries. Millions of capillaries carry blood between your veins and arteries. They reach into every part of your body.

Plasma
Plasma has a color like straw.

Red blood cells
These make up almost half of all your blood.

White blood cells
These make up only a tiny fraction of all your blood.

Your body has 60,000 miles (96,000 km) of blood vessels in it.

Plasma
Just over half your blood is made up of a substance called plasma. Most of the plasma is water.

Blood vessel walls

The walls of your veins and arteries have three main parts. Inside is the lining; outside is the outer coat. In between there is muscle.

Capillary
Capillaries have very thin walls.

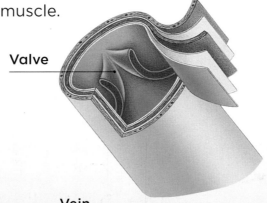

Valve

Vein
Valves in some veins stop blood flowing backward.

Artery
Muscles in an artery's wall help push the blood along.

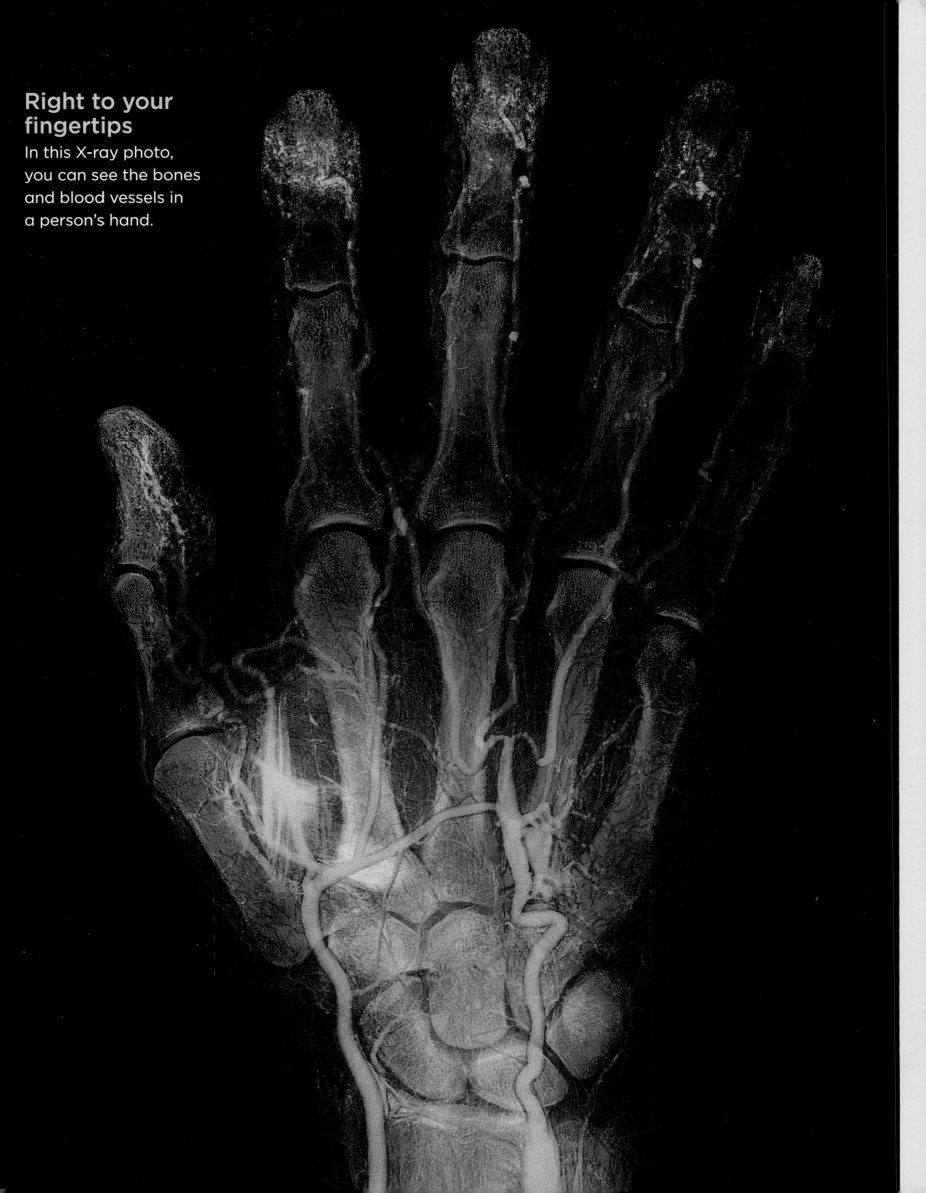

Right to your fingertips

In this X-ray photo, you can see the bones and blood vessels in a person's hand.

The body's pump

Your heart is in your chest. It is a bag of muscle about the size of your fist. It works all day and all night to pump blood through all parts of your body. It pushes blood into tubes called arteries. The arteries carry blood away from your heart. Smaller tubes, called veins, bring blood back to your heart. Then it goes around again.

Beating heart
If you place your fingers on your wrist, you can feel a steady beat. That is your heart pumping blood through your body. When you are exercising, your heart works harder to pump blood more quickly and give you more energy.

Four parts

Your heart has four main parts: a left and a right atrium at the top, and a left and right ventricle below.

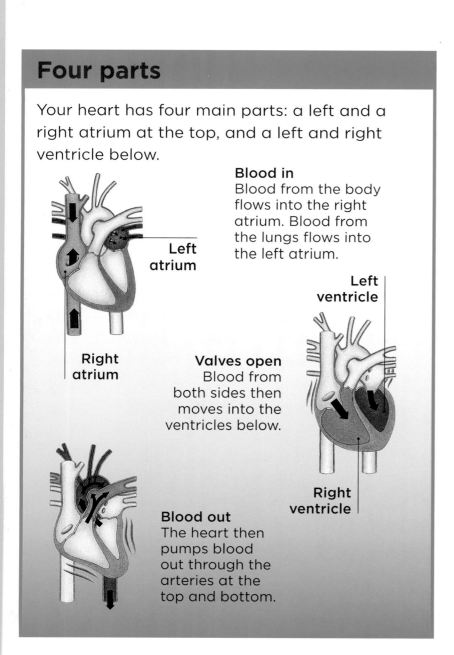

Blood in
Blood from the body flows into the right atrium. Blood from the lungs flows into the left atrium.

Left atrium

Left ventricle

Right atrium

Valves open
Blood from both sides then moves into the ventricles below.

Right ventricle

Blood out
The heart then pumps blood out through the arteries at the top and bottom.

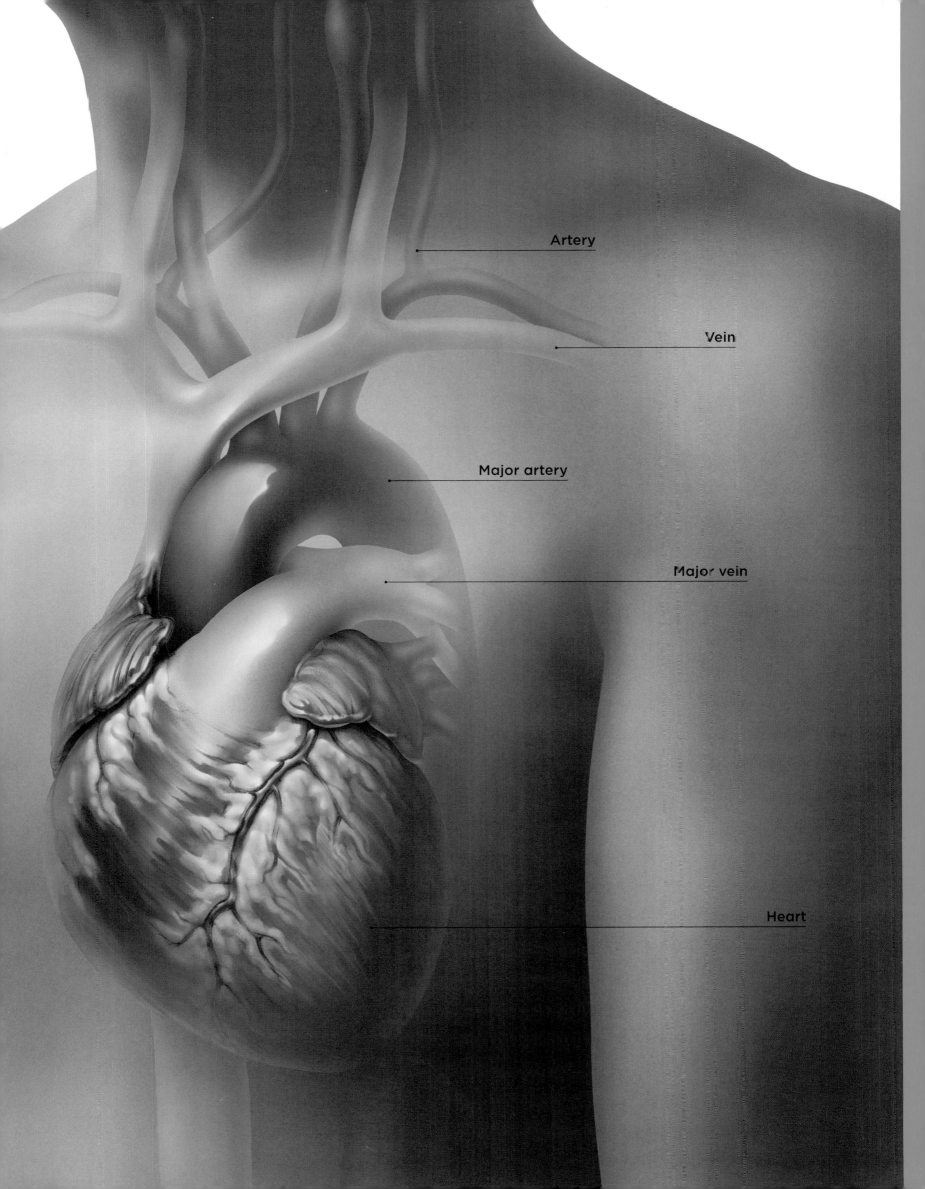

Artery

Vein

Major artery

Major vein

Heart

Breathing machines

If you try to hold your breath for long your brain will force you to start breathing again. We breathe in to get oxygen that our bodies need. We breathe out to get rid of carbon dioxide. When we breathe, we draw air into our lungs. The oxygen in the air then passes into our blood, which takes it through our bodies.

Each of your lungs has more than 300 million air bubbles in it.

YOUR BREATHING MUSCLE

When you breathe in, air goes through the nasal cavity in your nose, then down your windpipe into your lungs. The muscle below your lungs is called your diaphragm. It is your breathing muscle.

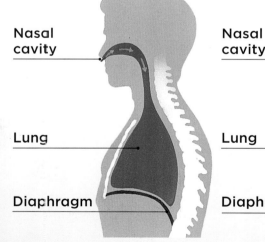

Nasal cavity

Lung

Diaphragm

Nasal cavity

Lung

Diaphragm

Breathing in
When you breathe in, your diaphragm goes tight and flat. It stretches your lungs downward and forward.

Breathing out
When you breathe out, your diaphragm springs upward and squeezes air out of your lungs.

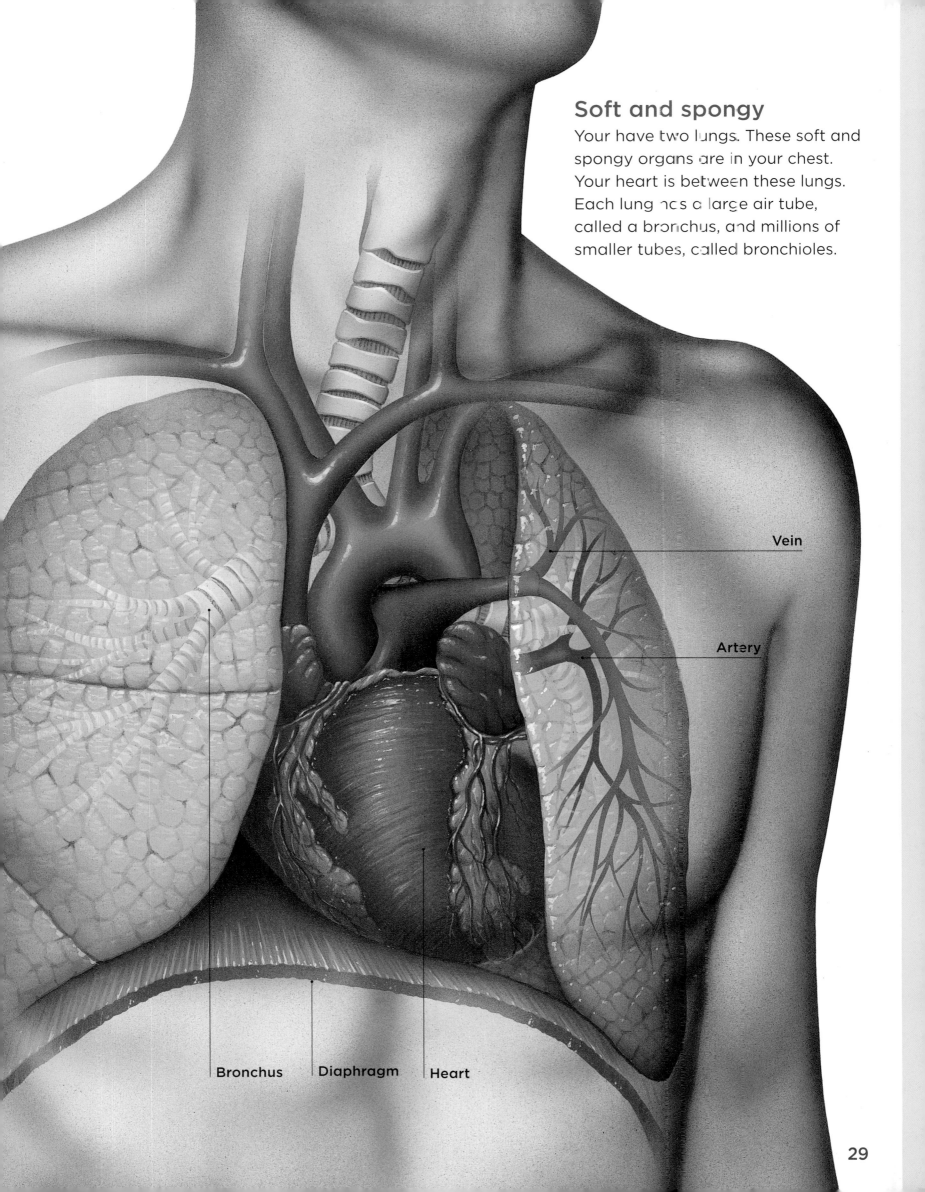

Soft and spongy

Your have two lungs. These soft and spongy organs are in your chest. Your heart is between these lungs. Each lung has a large air tube, called a bronchus, and millions of smaller tubes, called bronchioles.

Vein

Artery

Bronchus   Diaphragm   Heart

Brain in control

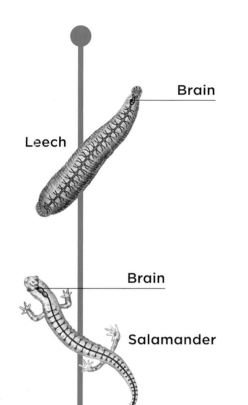

Brain

Leech

Brain

Salamander

Owl

Cat

Human

Your brain is the control room for all of your body. It controls what you see, hear, taste, smell, and feel. It tells you when you are hungry or thirsty. It allows you to think, dream, remember, and work. Nerves carry messages from your brain to all parts of your body.

Two parts

Your brain has two main parts, called hemispheres. About 100 million nerve fibers run between them. As the picture shows, different parts of your brain control the ways you see, hear, feel, and act.

> Your brain weighs about 3 pounds (1.4 kg), but it controls all your body.

Different brains

Human beings are more intelligent than other animals. Their brains are more complicated than the brains of cats, dogs, or owls. Some animals, such as salamanders and leeches, have very tiny, simple brains.

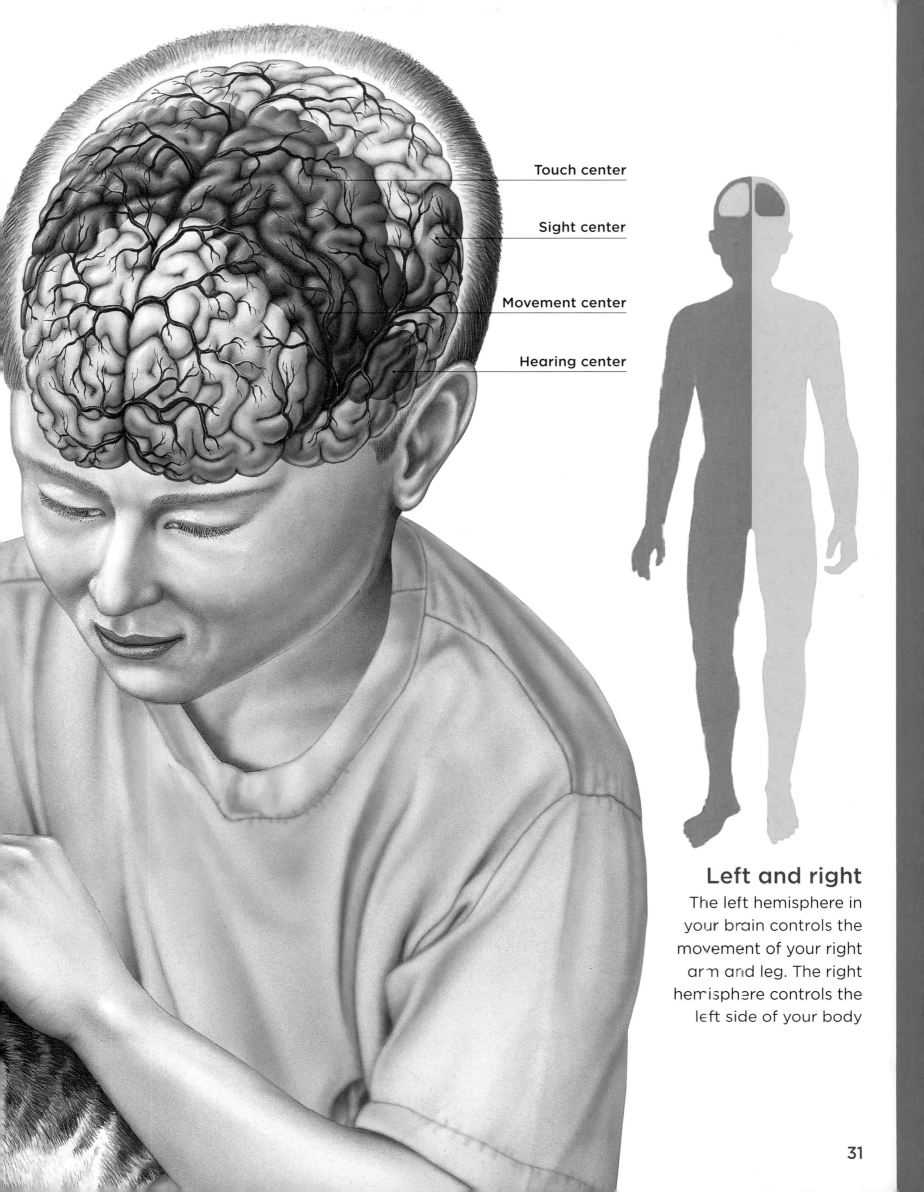

Touch center

Sight center

Movement center

Hearing center

Left and right

The left hemisphere in your brain controls the movement of your right arm and leg. The right hemisphere controls the left side of your body

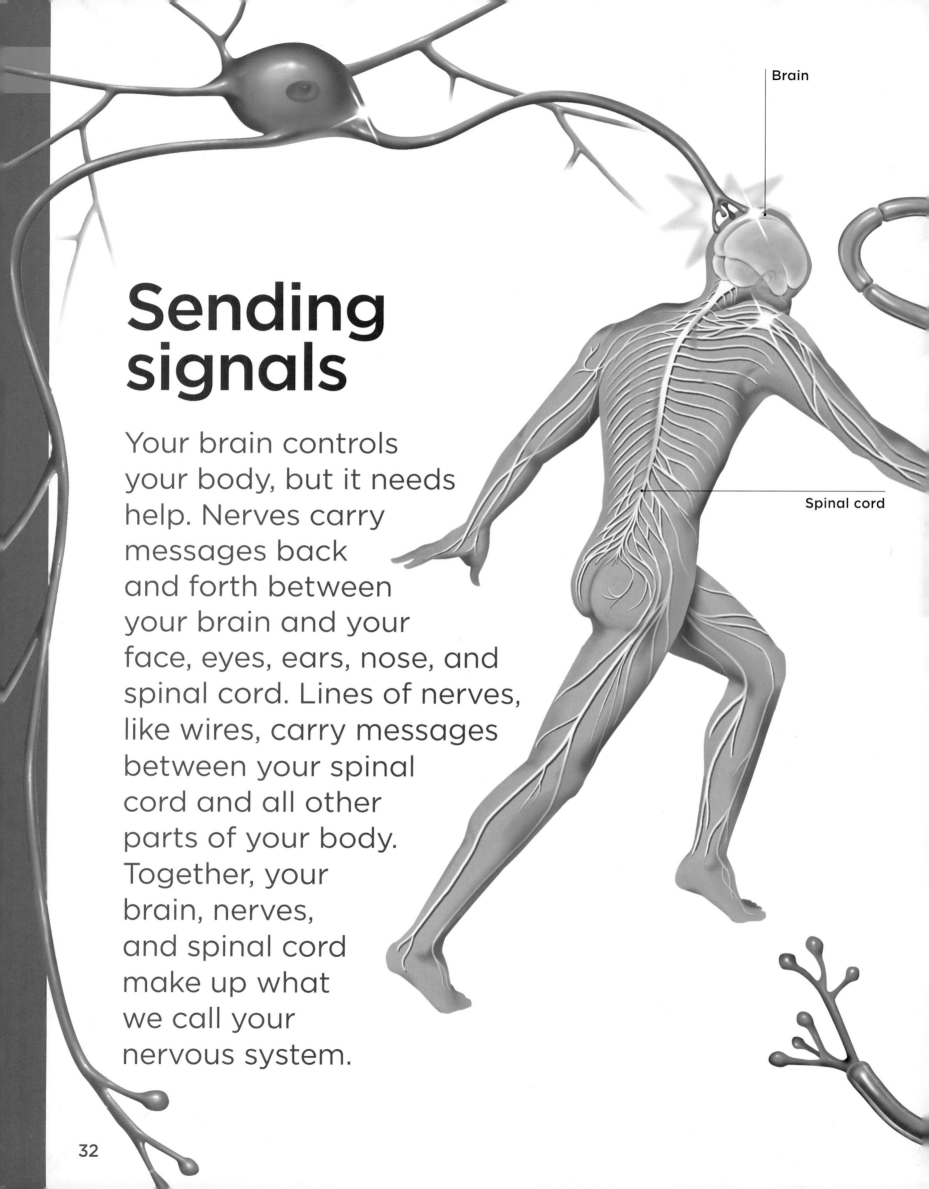

Sending signals

Your brain controls your body, but it needs help. Nerves carry messages back and forth between your brain and your face, eyes, ears, nose, and spinal cord. Lines of nerves, like wires, carry messages between your spinal cord and all other parts of your body. Together, your brain, nerves, and spinal cord make up what we call your nervous system.

Brain

Spinal cord

Nerve cells are called neurons. An axon is a neuron's long arm.

Interneurons pass messages within the spinal cord and the brain.

Synapses are gaps between nerves.

ACTING WITHOUT THINKING

If you see an angry dog or a house on fire, you decide to keep away. But sometimes you act without thinking. Your nerves act to keep you out of danger. If you touch something hot, you pull your hand away automatically. If something hits your knee, your leg springs upward. These actions are called reflexes.

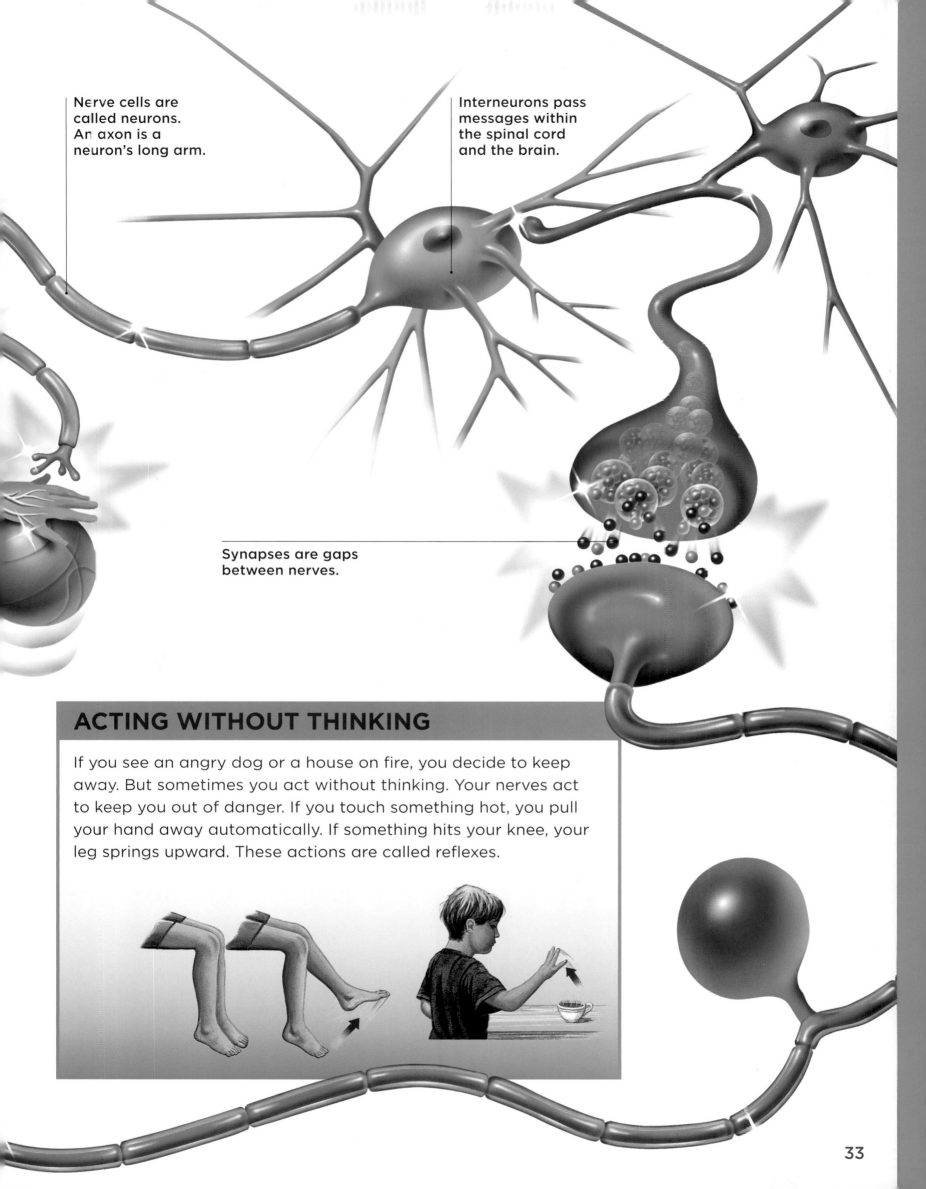

Seeing

You see things through your eyes. Light bounces off an object in front of you. This light enters your eye through the pupil—an opening in the center of each eye. It is like a camera. The light then falls on your retina—the back part of your eyeball. Nerves carry messages to your brain, which then lets you see the object in front of you.

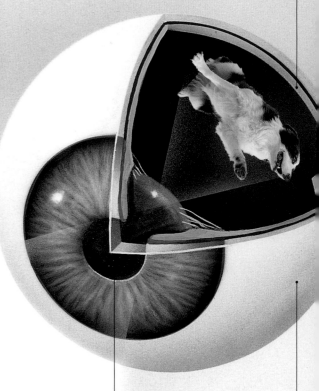

Retina
A picture of what you are looking at appears upside down on your retina.

Pupil
Light goes into your eye through the pupil.

White part
The outer part of each eyeball is covered with a tough white substance.

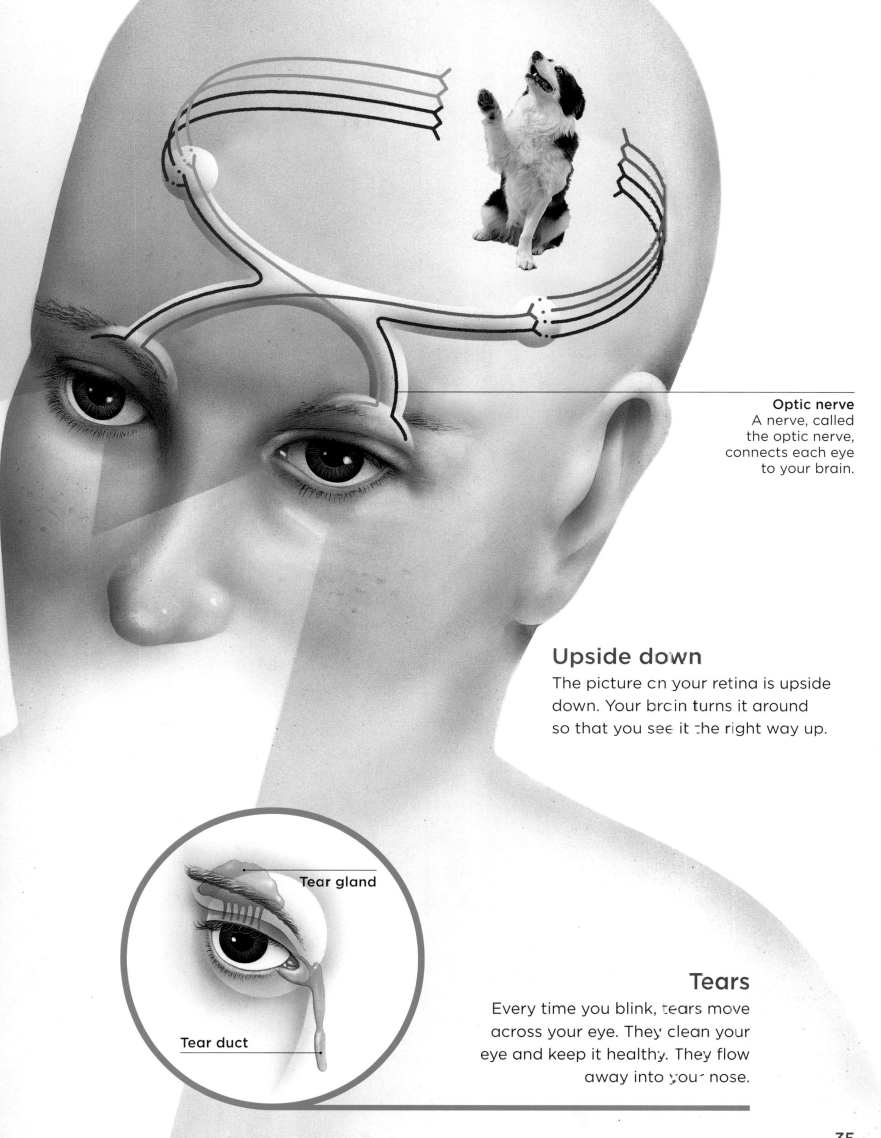

Optic nerve
A nerve, called the optic nerve, connects each eye to your brain.

Upside down

The picture on your retina is upside down. Your brain turns it around so that you see it the right way up.

Tear gland

Tear duct

Tears

Every time you blink, tears move across your eye. They clean your eye and keep it healthy. They flow away into your nose.

Hearing

Sounds travel in waves through the air. These waves enter your ear. They move down a passage and bounce off a piece of tight skin—your eardrum. When it vibrates, three tiny bones behind it move. They send the waves into another part of your ear—the cochlea. Nerves take messages from here to your brain. Then you hear sounds.

Three bones

The three bones behind your eardrum are the smallest bones anywhere in your body. They have special names.

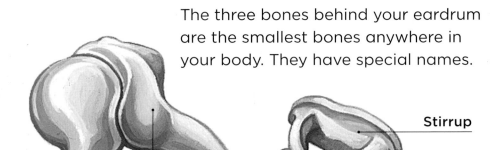

Stirrup

Anvil

Hammer

Dogs' ears

Dogs have wide, flat ears that can move. Their ears pick up more sound waves than our ears can. Dogs hear more sounds than we do.

Three parts

The part of your ear in front of your eardrum is your outer ear. The eardrum and the bones behind it are in your middle ear. Your cochlea is in your inner ear.

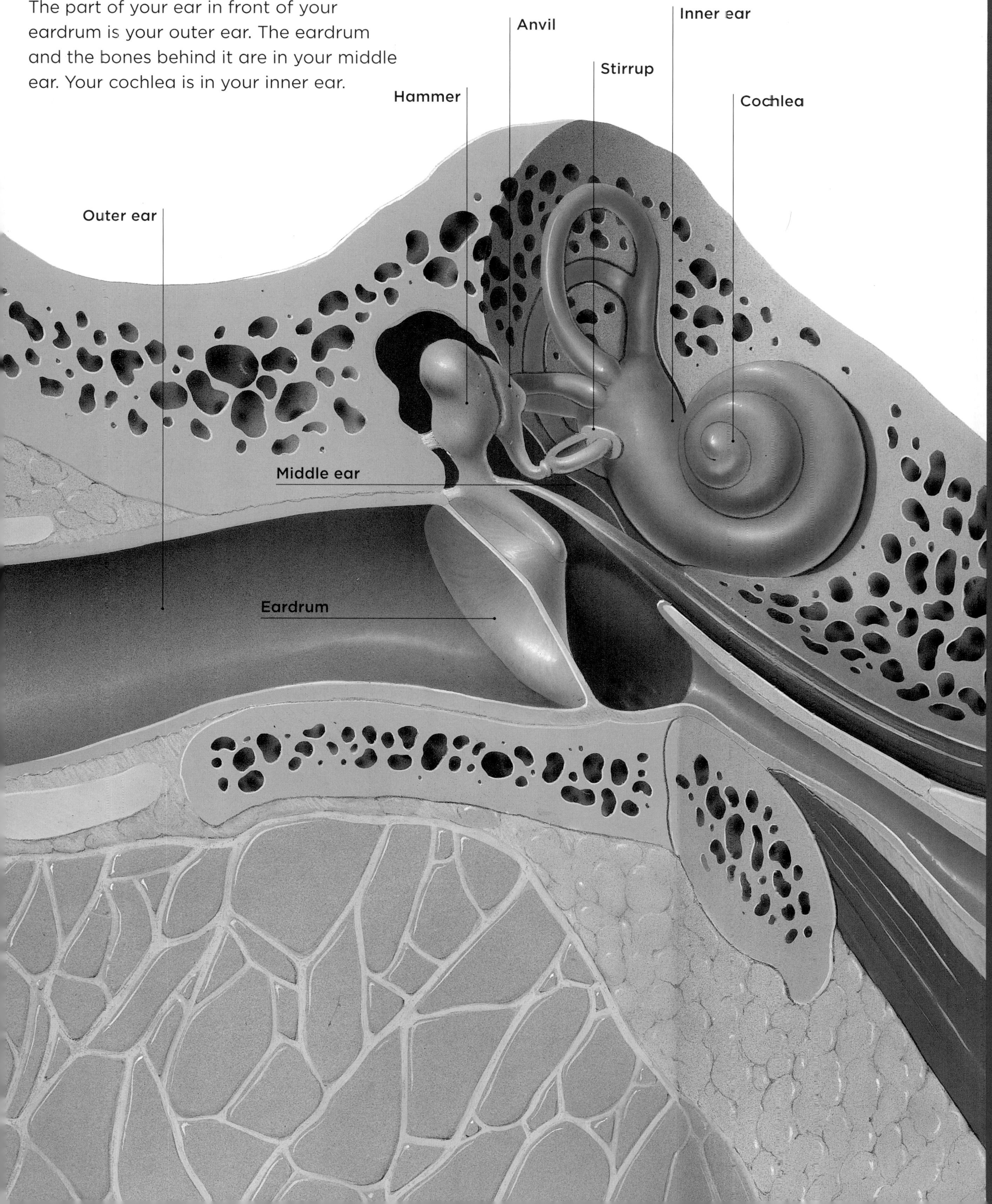

Anvil

Inner ear

Stirrup

Hammer

Cochlea

Outer ear

Middle ear

Eardrum

Smelling and tasting

Taste and smell are two of your five senses. Sight, hearing, and touch are the other three. The top of your tongue has more than 8,000 taste buds on it. These help you to tell different foods apart. At the top of your nose are two olfactory areas. You use these to smell lots of different odors—both nice ones and nasty ones.

Different nerves

There are taste centers and smell centers in your brain. Nerves carry signals from the taste buds in your tongue to your brain's taste centers. Other nerves carry signals from the olfactory areas in your nose to the smell centers in your brain.

Taste and smell

Taste and smell work together. Hold your nose when you eat chocolate, and see how different it seems.

FOUR FLAVORS

There are four main flavors in the food and drink that you taste. They are bitter, sweet, sour, and salty. Different foods have different mixtures of these flavors. The taste buds for sweet flavors are near the tip of your tongue. The picture shows where the taste buds for the other flavors are.

Bitter

Sweet

Sour

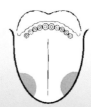

Salty

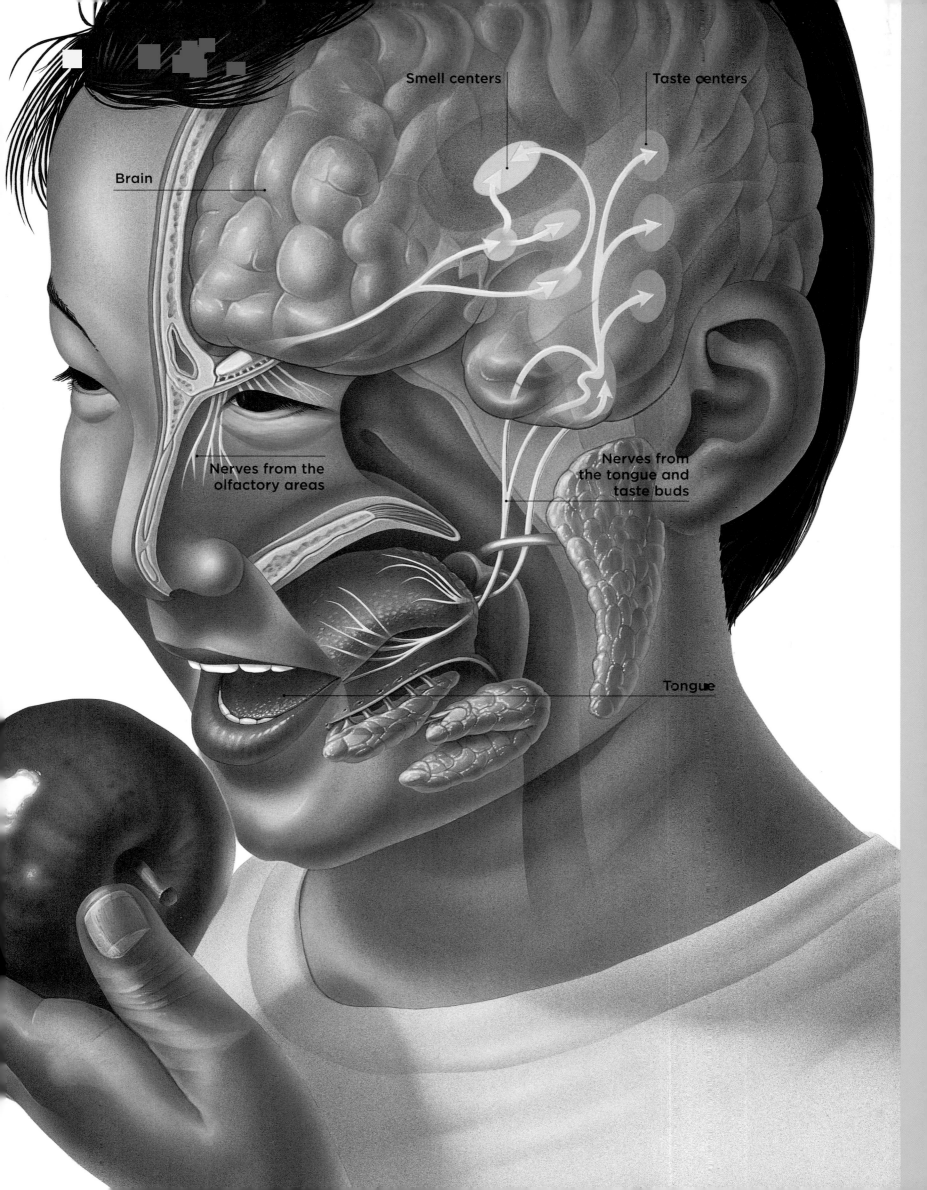

Smell centers

Taste centers

Brain

Nerves from the
olfactory areas

Nerves from
the tongue and
taste buds

Tongue

Eating

Food provides your body with the energy it needs to keep it working. When you put food in your mouth, you chew it with your teeth. Your tongue moves the food around and pushes it into your throat. From here, it moves down into your stomach. This chewed and mashed up food is then ready for its journey through your body.

THROUGH YOUR BODY

Large intestine

Small intestine

Stomach

Your stomach is like a bag with sides that can move out and in. It uses strong squeezing actions to break up food and force it into a long narrow tube—your small intestine. Some parts of this digested food then pass into a wider tube—your large intestine. From here they move to your rectum, ready to come out.

In your mouth

Your palate is at the top of your mouth. Your tongue pushes food against your palate. Saliva—or spit— comes from your salivary glands. It mixes with your food to make it soft and mushy before it goes down into your throat and then into your stomach.

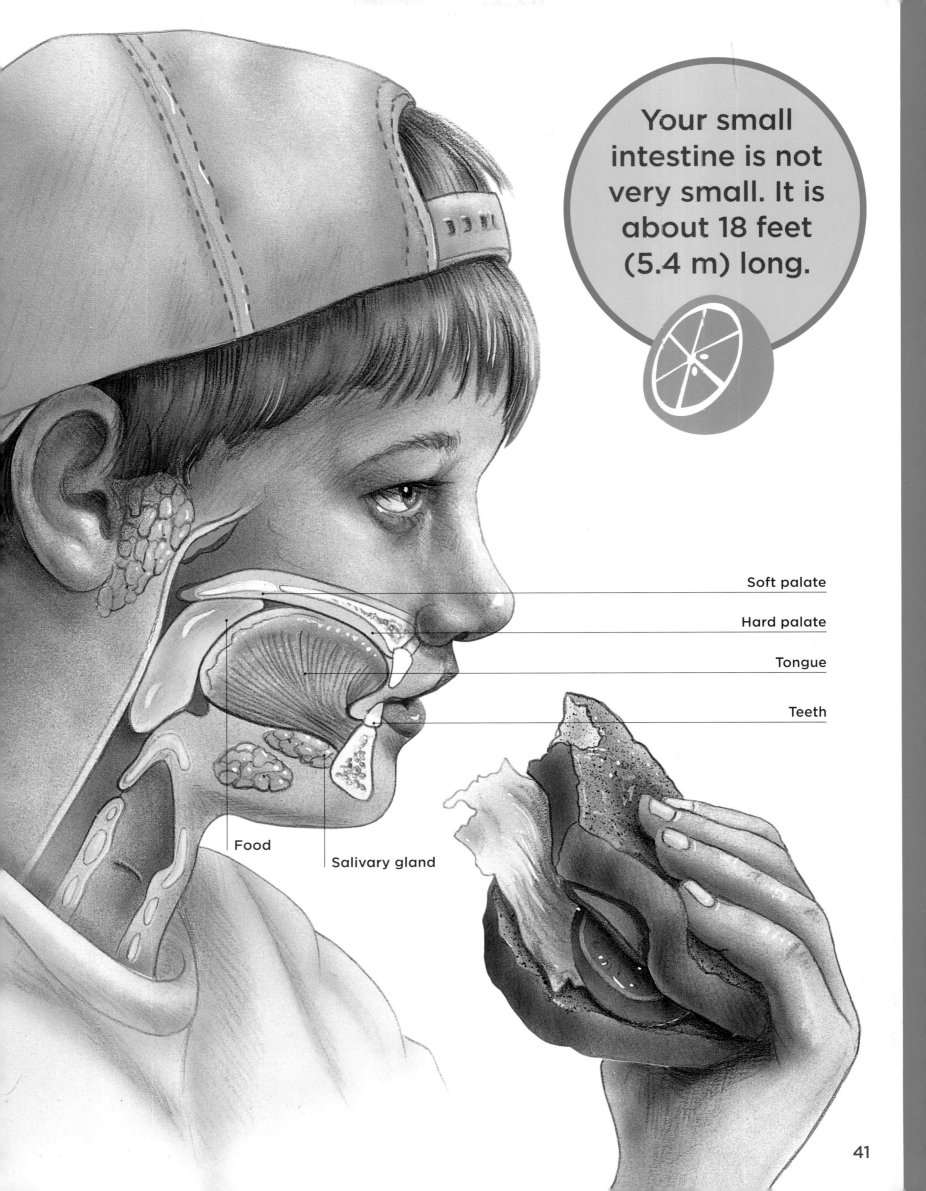

Your small intestine is not very small. It is about 18 feet (5.4 m) long.

Soft palate

Hard palate

Tongue

Teeth

Food

Salivary gland

Speaking

When you speak, you move your lips and tongue. You also move your vocal cords. These soft and springy bands are in your throat, near your larynx, or voice box. When air from your lungs flows over your vocal cords, they vibrate to make a sound. This is the sound of your voice.

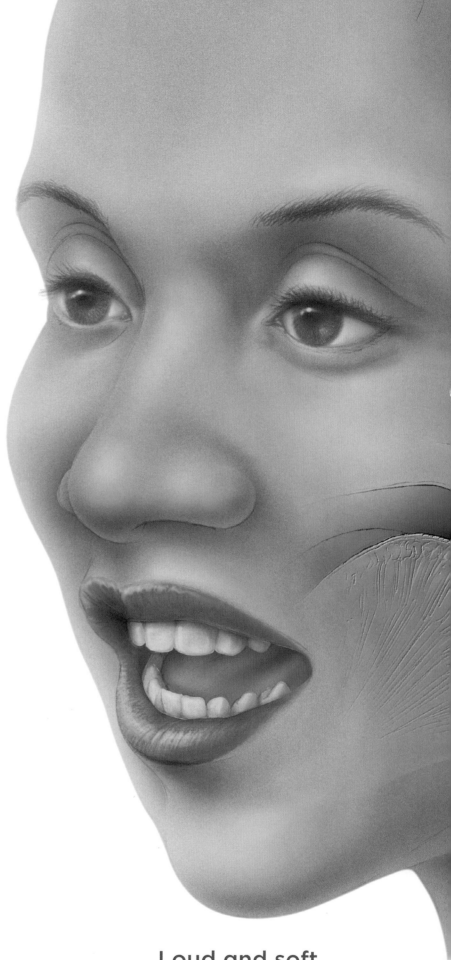

Shaping sounds

Your jaws, tongue, cheeks, and lips form different shapes to make different sounds. Some sounds are words. Some are just noises that we make.

Oooh

Mmmm

Aaah

Eeee

Loud and soft

When air from your lungs moves over your vocal cords very quickly, they vibrate to make a loud sound. When air moves slowly, your voice sounds softer.

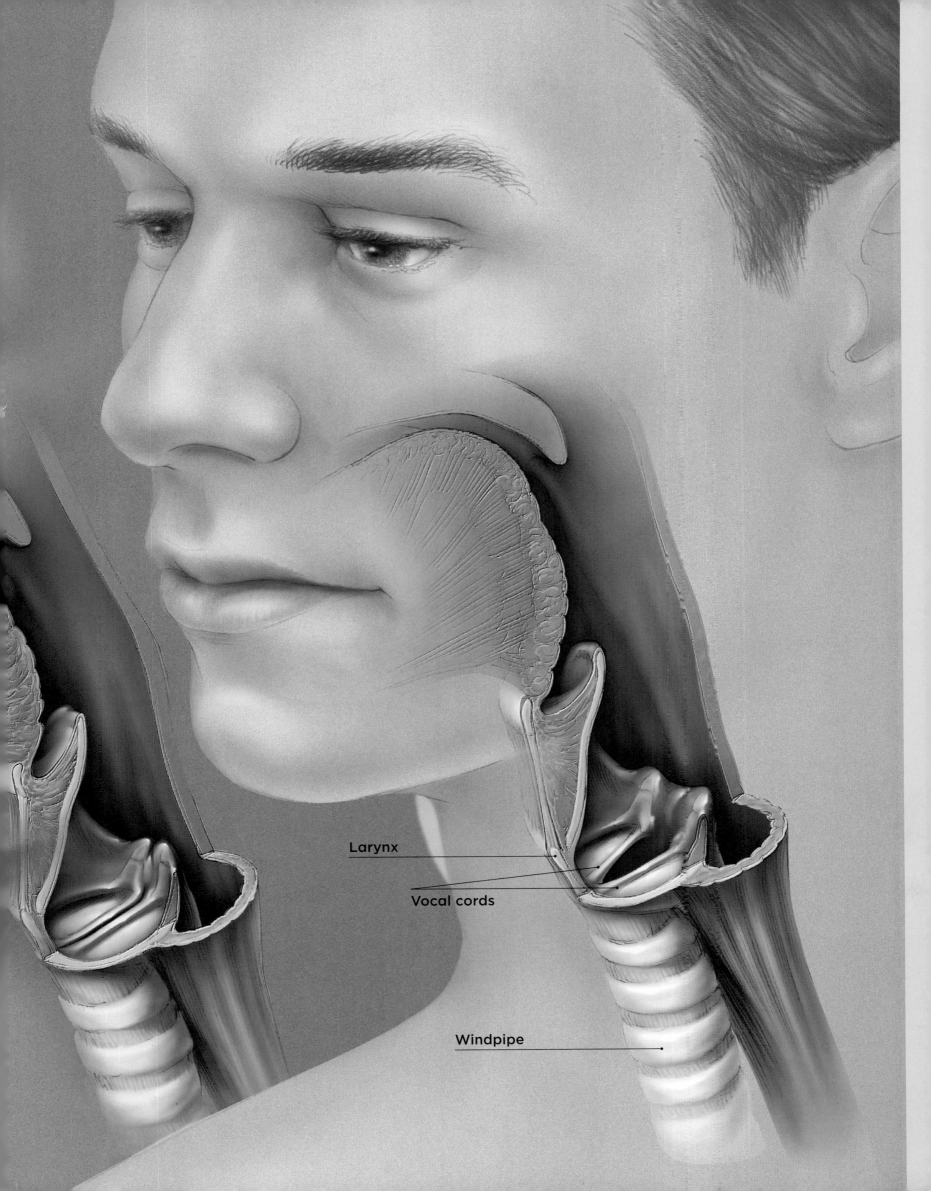

Larynx

Vocal cords

Windpipe

Growing up

Can you remember when you were three or four years old? You were smaller then. When you are about 12 or 13, you will be bigger than you are now, and your body will start to change. As you grow, your body becomes more active and you get better at doing lots of things.

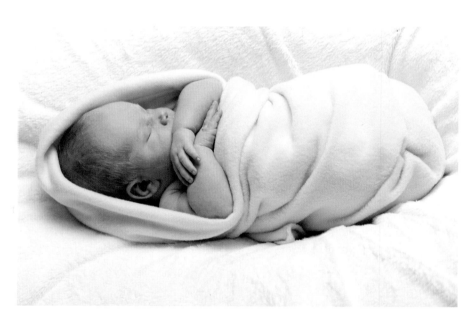

Baby

A very young baby cannot sit up by himself. Later he will be able to crawl, and after that he will learn to walk.

Getting better

The same boy drew these three pictures at different ages. His name is Sam. They are pictures of himself. You can see how the pictures got better as Sam grew older and more skillful.

Sam, age 4   **Sam**, age 6   **Sam**, age 8

Small child

A four-year-old child can walk, run, and jump. She can make friends with other children and talk and play with them.

Getting older

This 11-year-old girl is a very good reader. She can write stories and draw and paint interesting pictures.

Grown up

These 18-year-olds are now grown up. They will not grow any taller. We call them adults.

Glossary

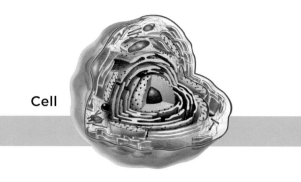

Cell

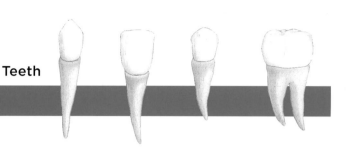

Teeth

arteries

Blood vessels that carry blood away from your heart

atrium

One of two parts in the upper part of your heart. Blood flows into these parts of your heart.

capillaries

The smallest kind of blood vessel. They reach to every part of your body.

carbon dioxide

A gas that we breathe out of our bodies

cochlea

Part of your inner ear. Nerves carry sound signals from your cochlea to your brain.

dermis

The inner part of your skin, underneath the epidermis. It contains blood vessels, nerves, and hair roots.

eardrum

A piece of tight skin in your ear that vibrates when sound waves strike it

enamel

A very hard substance that covers the part of your teeth above your gums

epidermis

The outside part of your skin. It is made up of hard, tough, dead cells.

intestines

Long winding tubes in your body. Food travels through your intestines after it leaves your stomach.

joints

Places where bones join together

larynx

The top part of your windpipe, where your vocal cords are

marrow

The soft substance inside your bones

melanin

A substance that gives your hair, skin, and eyes their color

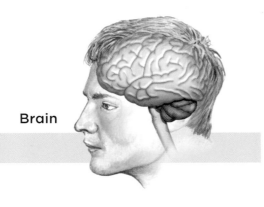

Brain

Muscles

oxygen

A gas in the air that you breathe in. Your blood carries oxygen to every cell in your body.

palate

The top part of your mouth. The front of your palate is your hard palate; your soft palate is behind it.

plasma

A substance that makes up just over half of your blood. Plasma is mainly water.

pore

A small hole in your skin. Sweat comes out of your body through pores.

pupil

A part of your eye. Light passes through your pupil into your eye.

reflex

An action you do automatically, without thinking about it

retina

The back part of your eyeball that allows you to see pictures of things you look at

skeletal muscles

Muscles that are attached to your bones

synapse

A gap between two nerve cells

veins

Blood vessels that carry blood from all parts of your body toward your heart

ventricle

One of two parts of the lower half of your heart. Your heart pumps blood out of the ventricles.

Index

Credits

Key t=top; l=left; r=right; tl=top left; tcl=top center left; tc=top center; tcr=top center right; tr=top right; cl=center left; c=center; cr=center right; b=bottom; bl=bottom left; bcl=bottom center left; bc=bottom center; bcr=bottom center right; br=bottom right

PHOTOGRAPHS

ADLIB=AdLibitum; iS=istockphoto.com; PL=photolibrary.com; SH=Shutterstock

Back cover br ADLIB (M. Kaniewski)

5tr SH **7**c ADLIB (M. Kaniewski) **9**tl PL (NIBSC/SPL) **11**c, tr ADLIB (M. Kaniewski) **12**bl PL (D. Bosler) **12–13**c ADLIB (M. Kaniewski) **15**tr, br PL (S. Peters) **18**bl ADLIB (M. Kaniewski) **19**br ADLIB (M. Kaniewski) **25** PL (V. Michaels) **36**br ADLIB (M. Kaniewski) **38**cr ADLIB (M. Kaniewski) **42**bl ADLIB

(S. Bowey) **44**c iS, tr SH **45**bl, r SH **47**tr ADLIB (M. Kaniewski)

ILLUSTRATIONS

Front cover Siri Mills tr, Marcus Cremonese bl, Kate Sweeney cl, Janet Jones br

Back cover Kate Sweeney tr

Susanna Addario **10**tl, **13**tr, **13**br, **14**c, **31**tr, **46**tr; Sam Burgess **44**b; Peter Bull Art Studio **8–9**c, **14**bc, **30**l, **46**tl, **47**tl; Leonello Calvetti/André Martin (photo)

3c, **22**tr; Marcus Cremonese **9**r, **24**tr; Dr. Levent Efe **8**l; Christer Eriksson **7**br, l **15**c, **23**, **34–35**, **35**bl; John Foerster **4**l, **26–27**, **42–43**; Peg Gerrity **41**; Gino Hasler **24**b, **26**bl; Adam Hook **6**bl; Janet Jones **16**br; Jeff Lang **36**cl; Siri Mills **7**tr, **32–33**; Spencer Phippen **36–37**; Trevor Ruth **6**r, **20–21**, **28**bl, **28–29**, **33**bl; Christine Shafner **19**tr, **17**br; Kate Sweeney **1**c, **16–17**t, **18–19**c, **21**br, **38**l, **39**; Rod Westblade **7**b, **10–11**b, **40**bl; Steve Weston **30–31**